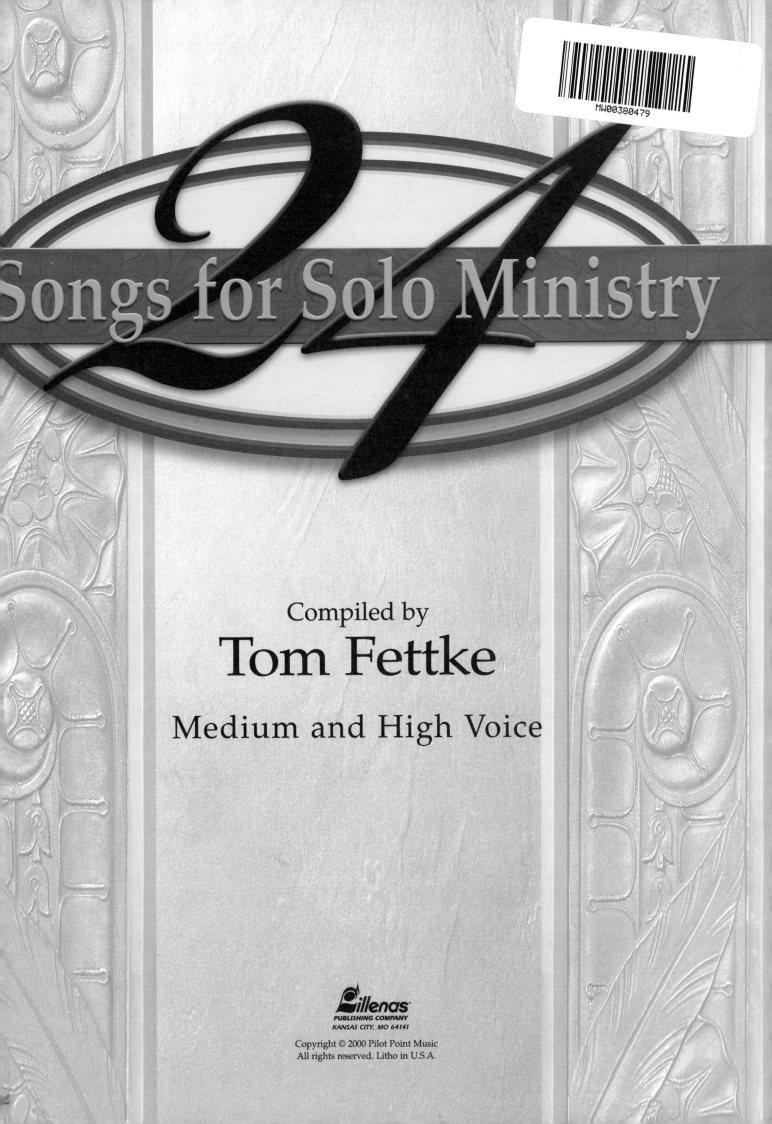

Songs for Solo Ministry

Compiled by

Tom Fettke

Medium and High Voice

Lillenas
PUBLISHING COMPANY
KANSAS CITY, MO 64141

CONTENTS

Be Still and Know

Words and Music by
STEVEN CURTIS CHAPMAN
Arranged by Tom Fettke

We Bring the Sacrifice of Praise

Words and Music by
KIRK DEARMAN
Arranged by Kyle Hill

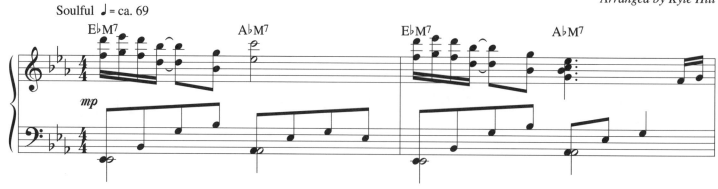

1. Lord, we've
(2. Lord, You've)

come in-to____ Your house and we've gath - ered in____ Your name;____ It's a
taught us in____ Your word to give thanks in ev - 'ry - thing,____ You'll pro-

How Beautiful

Words and Music by
TWILA PARIS
Arranged by Tom Fettke

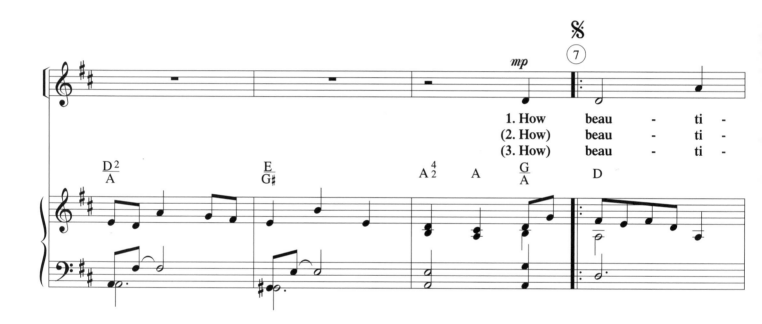

1. How beau - ti -
(2. How) beau - ti -
(3. How) beau - ti -

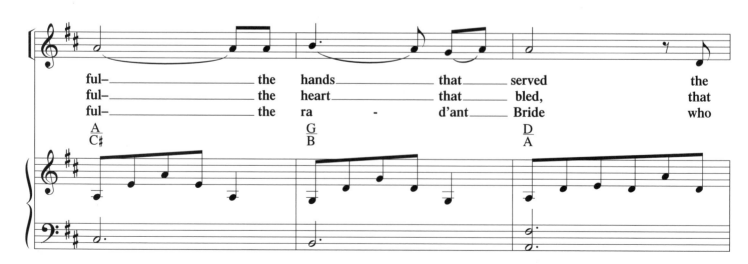

ful— the hands— that— served the
ful— the heart— that— bled, that
ful— the ra - d'ant— Bride who

PLEASE NOTE: Copying of this product is not covered by CCLI licenses. For CCLI information call 1-800-234-2446.

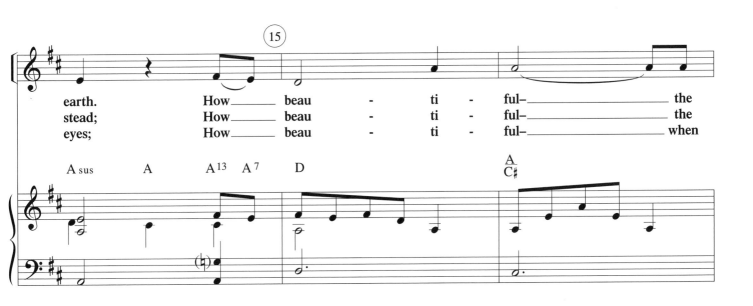

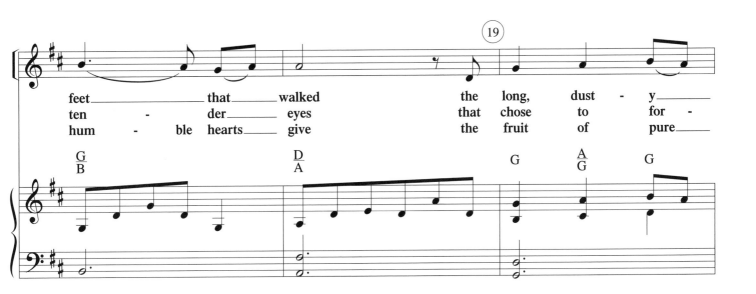

(to pg. 18, meas. 7)

When Answers Aren't Enough

Words and Music by
GREG NELSON and
SCOTT WESLEY BROWN
Arranged by Bruce Greer

Beyond the Open Door

Words and Music by
SHAWN CRAIG
Arranged by Gaylen Bourland

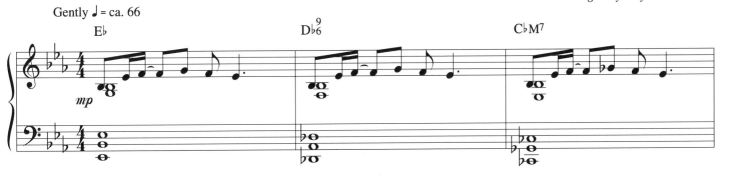

In the things____ fa - mil - iar we

find se - cu - ri - ty, Re - sist - ing all____ the chang - es that

Bow the Knee

Words and Music by
CHRIS MACHEN and
MIKE HARLAND
Arranged by Tom Fettke

Tenderly, with freedom ♩ = ca. 66

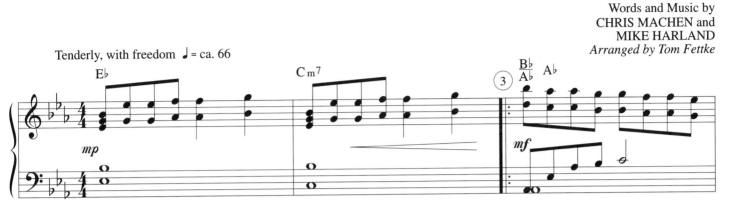

1. There are
2. There are

1. mo - ments on our jour - ney_____ fol - low - ing__ the Lord–
2. days when clouds sur - round us,_____ and the rain be - gins__ to fall,

Where
The

PLEASE NOTE: Copying of this product is not covered by CCLI licenses. For CCLI information call 1-800-234-2446.

In the Presence of Jehovah

Words and Music by
GERON DAVIS
Arranged by Marty Parks

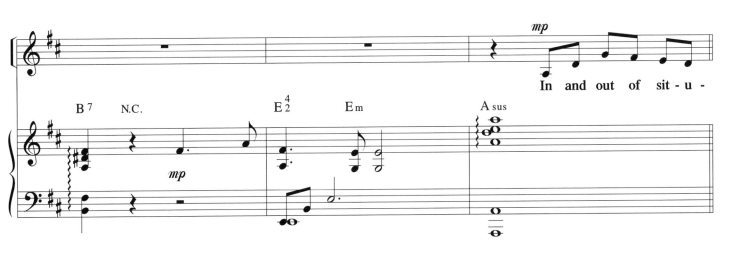

In and out of sit - u -

a - tions_____ that "tug of war" at me._____

Holy Ground

Words and Music by
GERON DAVIS
Arranged by Tom Fettke

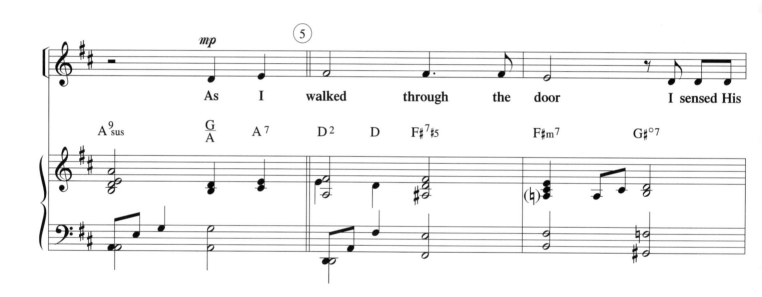

As I walked through the door I sensed His pres - ence,_____ And I knew this was the

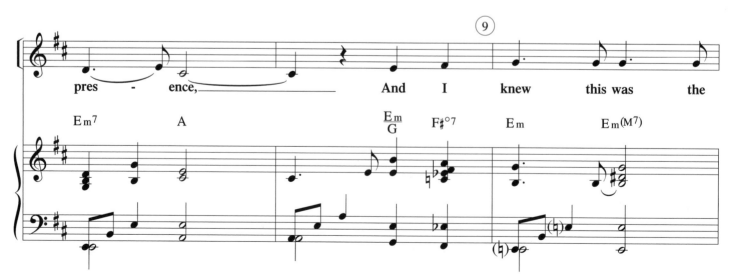

Honor and Praise

Words and Music by
TWILA PARIS
Arranged by Camp Kirkland

Righ - teous and ho - ly in___ all of Your___ ways,
Here to a - dore___ You for___ all of our___ days,

We come be - fore___ You with hon - or and praise.

Be Ye Glad

Words and Music by
MICHAEL KELLY BLANCHARD
Arranged by Bruce Greer

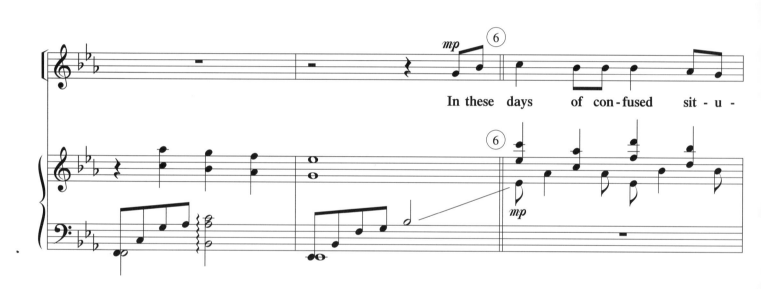

In these days of con-fused sit-u-

a - tions,___ In these nights of a rest-less re-morse; When the

had; O the love that your heart is now

tast - ing____ Has o - pened the gate, be ye glad.____ O be ye

glad! So be like lights on the rim of the

wa - ter,____ Giv-ing hope in a storm of the night; Be a

I Will Be Christ to You

Words and Music by
MARTY PARKS
Arranged by Marty Parks

In the name___ of Je - sus take my hand.___

I will be Christ___ to you,___

I will be Christ___ to you;___

I'll be His hands___ to do what I can,___ Be -

When Praise Demands a Sacrifice

Words and Music by
SUE C. SMITH and
RUSSELL MAULDIN
Arranged by Tom Fettke

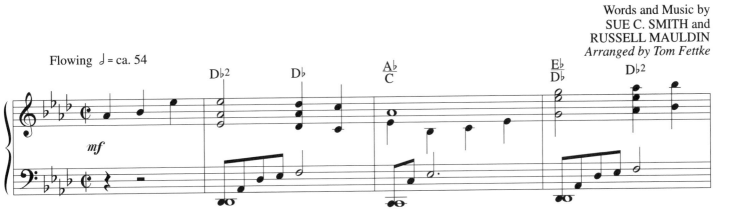

86

Reach the World

Words and Music by
MARK BISHOP
Arranged by Richard Kingsmore

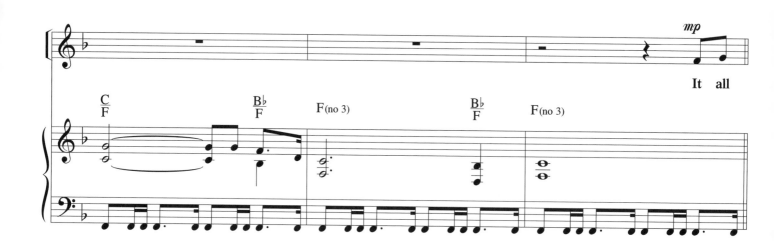

PLEASE NOTE: Copying of this product is not covered by CCLI licenses. For CCLI information call 1-800-234-2446.

96

Give Thanks

Words and Music by
HENRY SMITH
Arranged by Tom Fettke

Give thanks with a grate - ful heart.___ Give

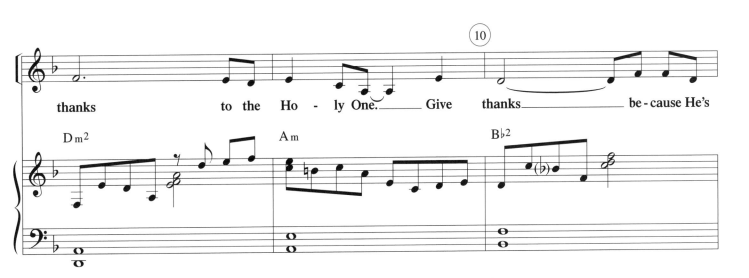

thanks to the Ho - ly One.___ Give thanks___ be - cause He's

Watch and Pray

Words and Music by
TWILA PARIS
Arranged by Bruce Greer

(to pg. 107, meas. 9)

hold the Bride - groom!

The Weight of the Cross

Words and Music by
CHRISTOPHER MACHEN
Arranged by Camp Kirkland
and Tom Fettke

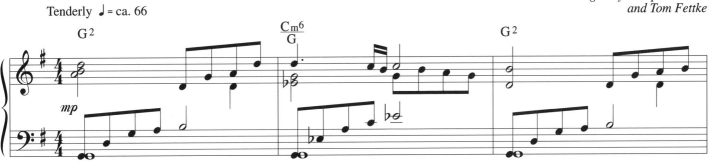

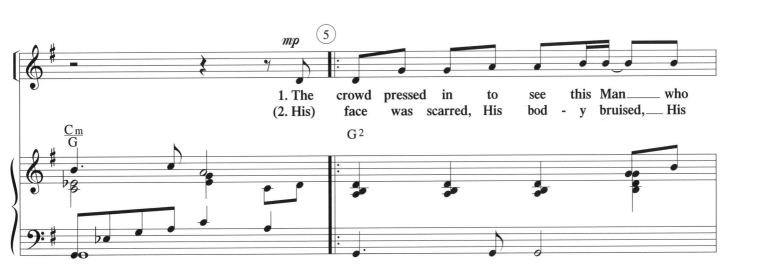

1. The crowd pressed in to see this Man____ who
(2. His) face was scarred, His bod - y bruised,____ His

stood con - demned____ to die, A Man they once pro - claimed as King,____ they
head was crowned____ with thorns, The crowd now jeered and cursed His name____ the

In His Presence

Words and Music by
DICK and MELODIE TUNNEY
Arranged by Richard Kingsmore

It's Still the Cross

Words and Music by
NILES BOROP, MIKE HARLAND,
LUKE GARRETT and BUDDY MULLINS
Arranged by Camp Kirkland

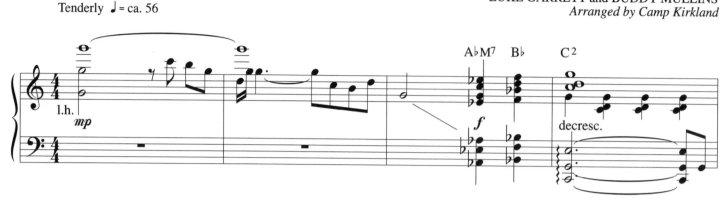

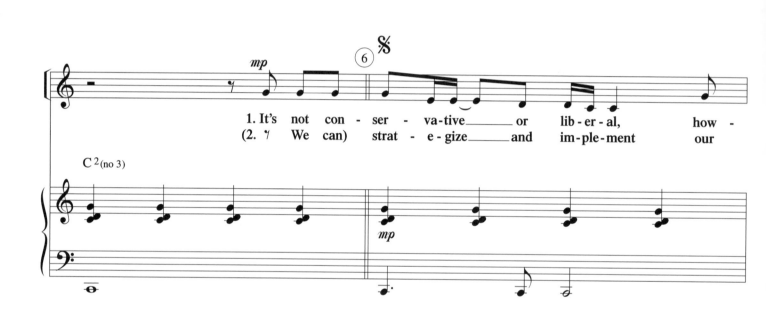

1. It's not con-ser-va-tive____ or lib-er-al, how-
(2. We can) strat-e-gize____ and im-ple-ment our

ev-er they're___ de-fined; It's not a-bout in-ter-pre-ta-tions or the
stanc-es and___ de-crees; We can con-trol our in-sti-tu-tions, ap-

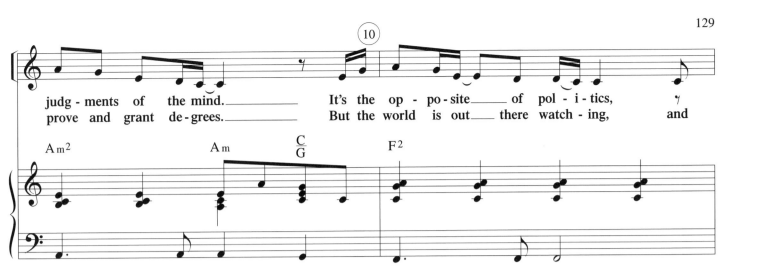

judg - ments of the mind._____ It's the op - po - site_____ of pol - i - tics,
prove and grant de - grees._____ But the world is out____ there watch - ing, and

pow - er and pres - tige._____ It's a - bout a sim - ple mes - sage and
what they need from us_____ Is to see our ris - en Sav - ior re -

wheth - er we be - lieve._____ It's still the cross, It's still the
flect - ed in our love._____

(to pg. 131, meas. 27)

Peace in the Midst of the Storm

Words and Music by
STEPHEN R. ADAMS
Arranged by Russell Mauldin

Desire of My Heart

BEVERLY DARNALL

JEFF SLAUGHTER
Arranged by John Darnall

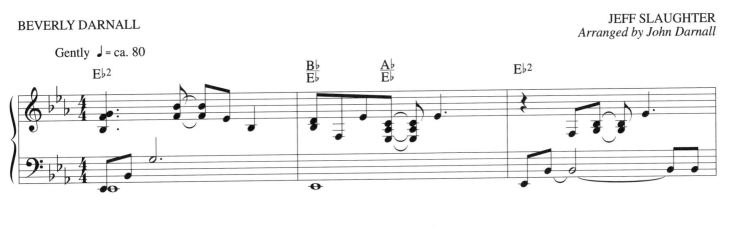

142

Prince of Peace

Words and Music by
TWILA PARIS
Arranged by Bruce Greer

Steady, with expression ♩ = ca. 94

1. There is no hope_____ for a world that de - nies_____ You,
2. There is no peace_____ for a new gen - er - a - tion

Firm - ly be - liev - ing a lie,
Liv - ing and grow - ing in fear.

Take Your throne,_____ right - ful

Lord._____ Prince of___ Peace, come and

reign for - ev - er - more._____

(to pg. 143, meas. 5)

more.

come and reign. Set Your feet on the

moun - tain - top a - gain. Take Your

throne, right - ful Lord.

Prince of Peace, come and reign for - ev - er -

Broader ♩ = ca. 94

We Are Waiting on You

Words and Music by
KIM NOBLITT and
CHRIS SPRINGER
Arranged by Tom Fettke

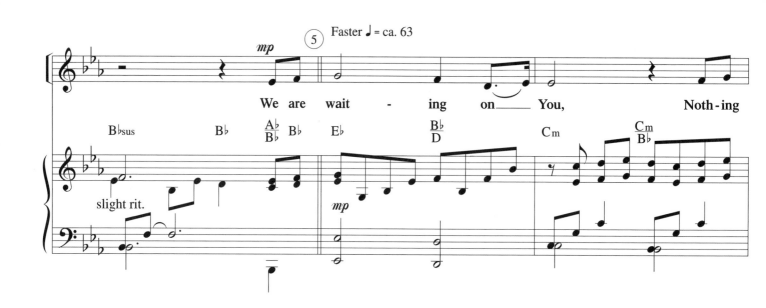

We are wait - ing on You, Noth-ing

else but Your touch will do. We've come to seek Your face, to

The Time Is Now

Words and Music by
TWILA PARIS
Arranged by Camp Kirkland

nev - er meant___ to make it on our___ own. The time is

day we face___ a choice that can - not___ wait. The time is

now to hear the call. From the Fa - ther of cre - a - tion comes an

an - swer for us all. The time is here, the time for you. If you

seek, then you will find___ Him, and the mo - ment that you do___ Seal your

heart with a sac - red vow.___ The time is

now.___

(to pg. 154, meas. 6)

vow.___ Now is___ the time and___ to -

When the Lamb Becomes the Light

Words and Music by
REGGIE HAMM and
JOEL LINDSEY
Arranged by Tom Fettke

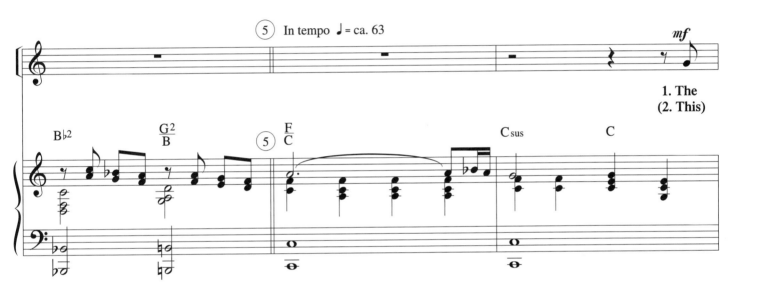

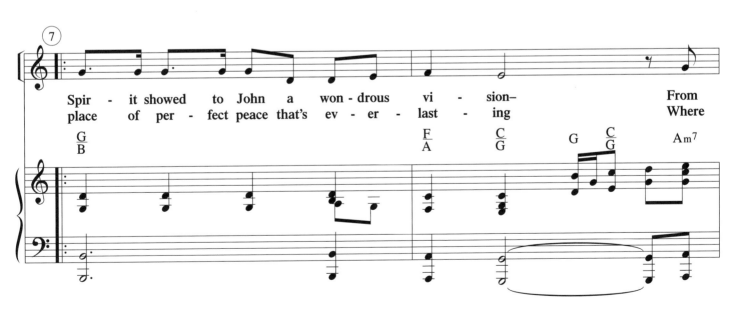